MW00453684

We hope you enjoy coloring this book.

Download some extra

free coloring patterns

and get news of upcoming books at

www.scribblepresscoloring.com/free-download

Made in the USA
Middletown, DE
19 December 2020

29335728R00038